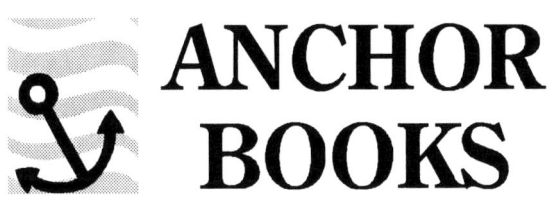
ANCHOR BOOKS

THE MIND'S ODYSSEY

Edited by

Neil Day

First published in Great Britain in 2000 by
ANCHOR BOOKS
Remus House,
Coltsfoot Drive,
Woodston,
Peterborough, PE2 9JX
Telephone (01733) 898102

HB ISBN 1 85930 850 3
SB ISBN 1 85930 855 4

FOREWORD

This truly inspired selection of poems are sure to delight all who read within. Featuring a variety of sonnets, villanelles and Rondeaux there is sure to be something for all lovers of the poetic form.

The book features a variety of themes from the delicacies of love, to nature and to the world and its toils around us. Each poem shows in style the true talent of each author as they share with you their own unique grasp of the poetic art.

Look no further for a fine collection of poetic form which will find a favourite place on your bookshelf.

Neil Day
Editor

CONTENTS

A LOST LOVE THE ENGLISH SONNET

Oh precious day, when you and I were one,
Your dress of pristine white with flowers of blue,
and I, in sober brown of cloth homespun.
Your face so eager, innocent and true.

Such precious nights exploring every kiss,
the days of leisure walking in the sun.
Your hand in mine, I knew no sweeter bliss
than of the thought that you were mine alone.

Summer days have fled and winds are cold.
Your face is paler now and sad your smile.
I hold you near, remembering summer's gold,
as close together we sit by the stile.

Sweet flowers of blue and white, for you alone.
I place them gently on your marble stone.

Margaret Walker

LOCKS OF GOLD

With locks of gold and eyes so bright,
She fills my heart, she fills my sight,
Her skin so fair, her gentle gaze,
I'm lost deep in love's sweet haze,
Sweet lips whisper in tones of light.

I reach for her, we touch, not quite,
Mere words lift me to divine height,
With waves of hair a spiral maze,
Her locks of gold.

I cleave to her, but try as might,
She drifts away into the night,
The yearning holds, my spirits raise,
She will return to still this blaze,
To bond to me in sacred rite,
With bands of gold.

Peter Walton

THE RED FOX

The red fox prowls in shadows grey,
As darkness falls she stalks her prey,
The crescent moon's pale shaft of light,
Befriends the hunter of the night,
Silently padding on her way.

Objectively she must display,
Cunning, slyness, without delay,
A well-earned meal is in her sight.
The red fox prowls.

The farmer's barn, she knows the way,
Survival for another day,
A snap of jaws, fleetness of flight,
Farmer's despair, vixen's delight,
He fires one shot, it goes astray.
The red fox eats.

Helen Mitchelhill

FANTASY

'Tis all a fantasy I fear, this earthly stay
Albeit not forever and a day
But who would want an endless journey's run
Observe each waning moon and rising sun
Sea-watch the flow of tides across the bay?

We dance our springtime through with sport and play
Enjoy sweet summer's laughter making hay
Youth vanishes and with it goes the fun
'Tis all a fantasy I fear

The autumn gold of life fades into grey
Fast comes the winter chill, how then to pray
That burden of all pains shall soon be done
Our dream is over 'ere it has begun
The piper calls the tune for which we pay
'Tis all a fantasy I fear.

Marion P Webb

WE ARE THE BEGINNING

We are the beginning of life.
To the end of the world's insight.
We are the dreaming kingdom shown.
The ancient land we call our own.
With endless love from dark to light.

We are the first who brought great might.
We are the last to stand and fight.
The last war won before we're home.
         . . . We are the beginning.

A new world gloriously bright.
Nations judged and set free with right.
We shall see how the world has grown.
The life and time it holds alone.
We will rise up and take to flight.
         . . . We are the beginning.

Heidi Welch

DELUDED, NOT KNOWING ONESELF

I didn't hear a single word
Words from a wise man went unheard
I chose to walk down my own path
The road was heavy with no map
Blistered soul, no goal, a sheep blurred.

If only I didn't feel dim
Hardly any bright spells shine in
Your words were spoken loud and clear
I didn't hear.

Thick symbol, still single, has been
Alone in the shade, rancid dream
For all that it's worth it's been worse
Uplifting spirit take this curse
Once independent, now need queen
I didn't hear.

John Beals

BLACKTHORN WINTER - A RONDEAU

Snow falls gently on frosted grass
Cold blackthorn winter's breath has passed.
Daffodils droop towards the ground
Where frozen primrose flowers are found.
Black ice has turned the pond to glass.

When sun breaks through the clouds at last
Warming this Arctic icy blast
Spring will return, but now around
Snow falls gently.

Will shepherds; scarlet skies forecast
To birds and beasts that winter's passed
Will rabbits huddled underground
Soon heard the birds' dawn chorus sound?
Now yellow storm clouds come, alas
Snow falls gently.

Audrey G Willis

WE HAVE A CHOICE

We have a choice as vigour wanes
When growing older - body pains
To try and overcome the fear
Of feeling litheness disappear
And dulling of once fertile brains

Is it wise to bemoan our strains
'Til nothing of life's joy remains
So all that we behold seems drear?
                We have a choice

If the heart gratitude contains
In spite of time making harsh claims
Contented thoughts will sweep woes clear
Leaving a path of peace and cheer
                We have a choice!

Tina Lipman

UNTIL SHE CAME

Until she came the man was mine,
For me alone his kiss divine,
How foolishly I thought he'd stay
In love forever and a day,
As constant as the stars that shine.

We used to drink of passion's wine,
Our bodies nightly intertwine,
Too much in love to break away,
Until she came.

Inviting lips he'd not decline
So stole his love, left me to pine,
Her smile had lead his heart astray,
Alone I dream of yesterday,
How once we shared a love sublime,
Until she came.

Ailsa Keen

JEUX D'ENFANTS

'Enjoy our games and try some more,'
The motto for our fun galore:
It's roundabouts and swings for us,
And slides and sandpits in the dust.
Why haven't we thought of this before?
Enough to make our parents roar
As over them cold bubbles pour.
We make a scene so riotous
As we enjoy our games.

It's good outside down on the shore,
But some prefer an indoor floor,
For some games can be serious
And give us a new stimulus
For leisure hours. There's always time for more
As we enjoy our games.

Gwilym Beechey

IT ENDS TODAY

It ends today, becomes decay,
The world turns itself a new way,
Time stands still as the image fades.
Inside hope's shattered, broken face,
Forgotten prayers see truth fall away.

And those who felt the need to pray
Silently watch their demise of faith,
the night to see the price to pay,
It ends today.

We see the light, know we can't stay,
Exist in fear of what will and may,
Realise that there is no escape,
Cage bars simply obliterate,
The key is locked where dead dreams lay,
It ends today.

Helen Marshall

JUST A MEMORY

Are we nothing but memory, you and I?
speeding along through a place in time.
While birds sing soft mellow song,
the wind ever blowing, never still,
sunlight beams spread her welcome warmth
onto others who will take our place.

Fleeting moments, speck of dust, then gone
life will continue along her evergreen,
but we all came for just a while,
now a memory.

Sharing our hopes wishing for dreams like all,
time passes, like the speed of light.
We found ourselves drifting into the skies,
forever gone we will be no more,
just a memory!

H Lewis

THE WATCHMAN

The cauldron suitor bore my love away;
Her shroud, the cold caress of ebb and sway;
whilst unrelenting tongues erode my home,
and mock me with her face amidst the foam.

I sometimes hear her weep beneath the chalk,
where once, upon its crest, I saw her walk -
- what beauty I beheld through fading light -
- one moment captured in unending night.

Though tempest fingers lured her white attire,
I watched - constrained to cause her to retire!
Deceitful arms reached up and drew her nigh,
to cease the restless cauldron's wanton cry.

I watch and wait, at last to love bestow,
upon my love - a thousand years ago.

David Watts

WHAT IS LOVE?

Two hearts together beating as one,
That special feeling that bonds two together,
An endless love can never be undone,
For a love so strong will last for ever.

Love surrounds us during times of sorrow,
Helping us to come through the bad times,
Giving us the strength to face tomorrow,
And forgiveness for previous crimes.

Love helps us find joy and happiness,
    It bonds families together for ever,
It is the light beyond the darkness,
Love is the only thing that lasts forever.

In our dreams and hearts we find love,
Love is symbolised by flying doves.

Diane Ralph

THE PENNYWORT

An English Sonnet

Between the chunks of granite of the wall -
    Rich golden-brown, which warm in summer's sun -
Some minute scraps of soil had blown in all
    The gales with which the winter had begun.

They found a place in crannies in the cold
    Bleak weather, filling spaces which let fall
Their crumbs of old cement which could not hold
    The ancient deep-delved rock which formed the wall.

Then germs of plants blew in among the dust,
    Small grains which held new life fell on the soil
And living fibres grew into the crust
    Made firm by rain and sun and wind's hard toil.

Now shiny rounded leaves delight our eyes
As spikes of pennywort reach for the skies.

Mabel Helen Underwood

LOVE IS HERE, DON'T LOOK FURTHER

A 1000 dreams spin round inside my head
Of possibilities for you and me.
I gaze beyond the room to set us free,
And ponder each one as I lie in bed.
Flashing lights spin round inside my head.
Upon the cliffs we look towards the sea.
The ship takes us away, just you and me
To wondrous lands about which I have read.

Upon consideration I must say
The life we share is sweet, so good and true.
As long as you are with me every day
I never need to find another you.
I long to hear the words you have to say.
My charming baby speaks them: *'I love you.'*

Debbie Perks

To A Special Colleen, Miss Adele Laird

Gentle wee colleen of tender year and grace
As morning star alone awaits to greet the dawn
Your letters sweet anoint with smile my face
As rising sun doth bathe sleepy rosetted fawn
And caress dove of Peace in sunlit glade.
Where from emerald bower songbirds do sing
To enhance the vestiage of fairy ring!
Luminescent pearl dewdrops alas must fade
With break of dawn - fate hath ordained -
Where seen not long before amid elfin dance
No idle boast - of a poet in acclaim -
The legendary magical unicorn did prance
To leave him spellbound - akin to fayne
Bowing before a fairy Queen, Adele by name.

Gilbert

BEREFT

I feel deserted, surely I shall pine
until my love relents for one more chance.
What can I do to rectify her glance
to make her eyes once more look into mine?
For a tender smile she may hold my heart,
keep it exclusively for her own use,
I'll stay bereft without my poet's muse.
Alone I'm damaged, lost, drifting apart -
together we could shower friends with love,
making them warm from the heat of our joy,
showing that passion can share, not destroy.
To be hurtful and mean, we'd be above.

She's here - no sound can I make, I just choke -
her looks disregard me at one mere stroke.

Geraldine Bruce

HOLY SOUL'S SACRED HEART
(Dedicated to Martina Bowens)

Here is character and stamp a torrid
Seal upon the holy soul's sacred heart.
What images of Christ engraved start
The inner thoughts of holy soul to rid
The evil the unholy ram that bid
The Christ of eternal love to now part
With goodness? The chief scribes at once used art -
Fullness, sinful intention they hid.
In one moment Christ saw Satan alive.
'Of spirit these words are not quality,'
He said to them. Ah, their hopes took a dive.
'The commandments live and they qualify,'
Said Thaddeus rejoicing beside the Lord
The scribes did not lay down their crossed swords.

Edmund Saint George Mooney

SORE DAWN

The Earth awoke, darkness lost,
Light came forth, from sun above
Day began, begun what cost
Hours in front, will they have love?

Movement slow, the bed called back
It's too soon, why comfort lose?
A stretch may make your body crack
Then day ahead, your head not choose.

Morn the time our eyes awake
Brain to show our body change
Seeing now, last night's mistake
Mind know not, of beer, or range.

If morning needs a happy start
Even time, time to be smart.

Geof Farrar

LIFE EVERLASTING

News are a see-saw between birth and death,
Our world is part of a vast universe;
Millions of galaxies none can traverse.
Vast starry hosts widen wonders of truth,
Like mile deep Grand Canyon richer than wealth.
Heaven is here unseen by minds perverse,
It is love's power in selfless deeds diverse;
Friendship's full healing, pulsing from God's breath.

Jennifer faced death when a happy girl.
She pictured her grandma's smiles in heaven.
'Dear Ningma I often look at your pearl,
What fun and laughter when I was seven.
Mummy says banners of blessings unfurl,
Join us ever in love freely given.'

James Leonard Clough

HAPPY BIRTHDAY

Birthday greetings, three score years and ten they say,
You have reached three score years and twenty today,
Every day is, as we say
Truly another 'Bonus Day',
What more can we say?

I hope you will continue to enjoy life
With your dear and loving wife
Still visiting places where you like to go.
                              Birthday Greetings.

You are such a lucky guy,
You do so well with that one eye.
Although I know you're not a vegetarian
You are a super octogenarian,
And on my sincere good wishes you can rely.
                              Birthday Greetings.

Frances Jenkins

Darkness We Fear

Darkness we fear, strange forms we sight,
In torment, souls flit through the night,
Searching for what, we do not know,
Moans, groans, darting to and fro,
With sightless eyes, in restless flight.

No one knows the wherefores, or whys,
Spirits with their demented sighs,
They're unable to see us, even though,
Darkness we fear.

Crime, a lost love, why do they wait?
Adrift in limbo, this is their fate,
Do they exist, we cannot tell,
Nothing can free then from this hell,
These creatures of horror, of hate,
Darkness we fear.

Patricia Barrett

WHEN THEY'RE GROWN

In children's hearts the seeds are sown
For thoughts and actions when they're grown,
A father's praise, a mother's pride,
Encouragements which pace each stride
As they step out in life alone.

Some hearts are cold, as hard as stone,
Good friends are rare, no one their own,
But love if nurtured will abide
In children's hearts.

When childhood days have quickly flown,
With lessons taught and way now shown,
No parents near to be their guide,
To give advice or take their side,
Then lives are shaped from all things known
In children's hearts.

Avis Ciceri

I SEE DARKNESS

I see darkness behind your eyes
And hear your sad and fetid lies.
I long to rid you from my sight
And sell your soul to hell each night,
But Satan never hears my cries.

You fill my heart with dark despise.
I wish the truth would blind your eyes.
In your lifetime of pain and spite,
        I see darkness.

I cry to you, Lord of the flies,
To take the evil from my eyes.
The mirror fills my soul with fright,
And turns my hair to godly white.
I'm the demon, before my eyes . . .

Peter Steele

LOOK AT MY BILLS

Look at my bills and tell me what I can afford
I do my accounts with an economic chord
Every penny counted for how it is spent
Shopping or bills, no loan I'll be lent
This is the crisis that I have on board.

My financial crisis that I have on board
Look at how prices have soared
No regard for whether I can pay my rent
Look at my bills!

You fat cats there who can afford
Luxuries needless that who hoard
Greed which you do not repent
A sin which we workers do resent
Yet you ignore my pleading word
Look at my bills!

P Edwards

LIFE IS TO CHERISH!

Life is to cherish, come what may,
For months and years pass as a day.
A gift of love, nurtured with pride,
'Fore independence takes a stride,
Days, stealthily, fritter in play.

Childhood, youth, hold idyllic sway,
Milestones soon passed along the way,
Then man sees fit to take a bride,
Life is to cherish!

Mid-life clings, old age at bay,
Tomorrow just another day,
A sudden swamp by time and tide,
So many friends recently died,
Use to the full each new today!
Life is to cherish!

Pat Heppel

IN GOD WE TRUST

'In God we trust' we blindly say,
but yet we fear again today,
it seems our faith is not as strong,
as when the Lord first came along,
the fire in our souls melts away.

That certainty that came to stay,
Absconds when tested day on day,
like sheep we are all drawn along,
            In God we trust.

But protect us all Lord we pray.
and see us through this fearful day,
Let us now join your blessed throng,
take me to where my heart belongs.
Come to me without due delay,
            In God we trust.

Bill Hayles

SUCCESSFUL DEFEAT?

Write a rondeau! Give it a go!
Easy to say - that's all they know!
Leave it alone, much the best way.
Maybe I'll play some other day -
When will that be? Say, tomorrow?

Let's start again, go with the flow!
Stay with the theme - will it work? No!
Tomorrow's here, now it's today -
Write a rondeau!

Stare at the page, nothing to show.
Stuck in a rut. I'd like to know
Who started this? Some birdbrain, eh?
Drive us all mad! All right! Okay!
Do it yourselves. Why don't you go . . . !
Write a rondeau?

Pat Watson

MILLENNIUM HAPPENINGS

Today, time of war, hatred and kill,
Yesterday, fun, rejoicing, free will.
Millennium past, souls going too,
People passing away, at the liberty of who?
'Tis the steep climb of greed, filthy the hill.

Roads and homes with debris do fill,
Warfare should end, people flee until
Shouting, screaming mortal storms brew.
Today, time of war.

Offering of peace, no agreement still,
Stubborn politicians, minds poisoned, ill.
'Why shall we suffer at the expense of you?'
Families cry, both sides still have no clue.
A city destroyed, how high is the bill!
Today, time of war.

Parivash Jeelani

COMING DOWN TO EARTH

Coming down to Earth, truth brings shock,
Bids unidealistic mock;
Tint is heightened by fantasy,
Mind, like butterfly, light and free,
Artlessly plans its own epoch.

Whilst uniformity takes stock,
Reality's disciples knock
In vain; sweet absorption stops me
     Coming down to Earth.

Routine rules, marshalled by the clock.
Dare I make life's foundations rock,
Cock a snook at mediocrity?
Though there's security for me,
Pity deserter of the flock,
     Coming down to Earth.

Ruth Daviat

À CHEVAL (ON HORSEBACK)

A highwayman always wore a mask
robbing and thieving was his task
a horse - a tricorn hat - and a cape
Upon his steed in blackened darkness he waits
till stagecoaches over rough moorland pass.

'Hand over money and jewels - now - make it fast
Loaded pistol's ready - come on or it'll be your last.'
His partner Tom King was shot - was this fate?
                                        A highwayman.

Rode like Satan from London to York in one night
they say - just to get an alibi right.
Caught for horse theft - now it was too late
clamped in irons behind the prison gate
Turpin Richard (Dick) hanged 1739 - York press write.
                                        A highwayman.

David Charles

Time To Wake Up

Time to wake up, leave this dark night,
Now tears and sorrow are not right.
Despair and heartache must not grow
Lest senseless self-pity should show.
Brooding misery put to flight.

Think positive, use all your might,
Get out and about, use your sight.
Go, find some true friends that you know.
            Time to wake up.

Seek others in a far worse plight
The aching pain will then be slight.
Your loving heart to them will flow,
Take it easy, gentle and slow,
Leave this dark night for day is bright.
            Time to wake up.

Betty Broom

I Hear Feet Marching

How can it be I hear feet marching?
I'm alone in the unknown searching
Why has life lost all its joy?
While all the time there're pleasures to enjoy
I gaze through the window, see the crimson ivy cling.

The world is full of mortal sin
Throw the dice and hope to win
What's the use of dreaming, I want to sleep,
Through the breeze, I hear feet marching.

Full moon is floating through the clouds
Sometimes covered in a dark feathery shroud
I visualise sweet music from above
Echoes of a band playing *God is Love.*
I'm alone though I talk aloud
'Is there someone there?' I hear feet marching.

Frances Gibson

THUNDER

The storm has come, the sounds of war
Come from the mighty throne of Thor,
Along with lightning, swift and bright,
That navigates the evening light
And strikes the Earth's unyielding floor.
Above the storm's discordant roar
That shakes calm nature to the core,
Rain clouds invade the native night :-
The storm has come.

From the crack in heaven's door
Will come a hundred bolts and more
To put the evening's calm to flight,
Before the all-embracing might
Of the furious rage of Thor . . .
The storm has come.

Anne Rolfe-Brooker

LINES TO A CIRCUS VICTIM

We are to blame each time we turn
Our back when acts of cruelty learn,
Stifle the urge to intervene
And obviate the most obscene -
A goal for which we yet would yearn.

Trudy saw our anger burn
That she, a helpless creature, earn
Foul treatment dubbed much more than mean.
We are to blame.

Each time we stay quite taciturn
Through criticisms thought too stern,
Now know how false the justice been,
How little of it truly seen.
The rings remain, as those Saturn.
We are to blame.

Mary Ryan

I MOURN THE LOSS . . .

I mourn the loss of words unsaid;
Such happy lives we could have led
Had we been brave and confessed all,
Unworried what might then befall
Our partners we'd already wed.

Now what a lonely line I tread:
How shall my yearning heart be fed?
Since you'll not be there when I call,
I mourn the loss.

Had we declared our love instead,
A joyous ending might be read.
But fear of heading for a fall,
Too dear the price, and high the wall,
Leaves winters long, and summers dead . . .
I mourn the loss.

Phyllis Spooner

'RENOUNCEMENT' REVISITED
(After Alice Meynell)

I mustn't think of you. I'll do my best.
But it's so hard; you're always on my mind.
Watching the sky, hearing a song, I find
the memory of you won't let me rest.

You fill my happiest thoughts; I am possessed
by images of you, just out of sight.
I try to keep them out, my eyes shut tight,
but stopping short of you's a cruel test.

Though, when night comes at last, when I let go,
surrender my restraint to sleep at last,
loosen my will like clothes I put away
to lie in naked freedom, then, I know
in dreams I'll run to you, you'll hold me fast.
Nothing will part us then but break of day.

Joan Sheridan Smith

A CERTAIN WAY OF LIFE

It seems to be a certain way of life
To scream and shout, kick, knife and roundly curse
To take delight in beating up a wife
Enjoy as each succeeding yell sounds worse.

Raise the 'blaster to higher decibels
Stone the guardians of some impotent law
Threaten those whose soft words would break the spells
Of a way of life spilling blood and gore.

Four-letter words are the staple diet
But an officer knows therein lies the lies
Of the instigators of a riot
So he calms the screams down, to sobbing sighs.

A fawning plea cries 'Sir I'm only poor
My way of life is just to break the law!'

John Aldred

LUCY

I have a friend whose gentle shining face
Looks left and right and up and down the house;
Who treads so softly, moving with such grace
In search of food, or possibly a mouse.

She always wears a coat of finest fur
And rubs around your legs to let you know
She wants attention, then she starts to purr
And makes it very hard for you to go.

She washes all around and keeps so neat,
And dashes here and there to have some fun;
She's fussy over what she has to eat,
Then sleeps for hours until the day is done.

Oh, how much I love my little Lucy,
A friend for life, my dearest faithful pussy.

Anthony Manville

FROM FRIEND TO LOVER

Will you my friend, the one I love
Be forever my own, even unto eternity's end?
Let my affection cover you like a dove
I need to be more than just your friend.

I have known you, but a little while
Yet I know you are mine
I know your face, your lips, your smile
How long must I walk the line?

You keep me at a distance, keeping me apart
Knowing how I feel, and holding you dear
Can you not feel my tender, true, loving heart?
Am I losing you? That much I fear.

All is not lost, for your love is true
All is well, for I adore you.

G Bannister

BEREFT

'Distance can't divide us' I hear you call
You graced this poor existence from the start
Like a storm at sea, the torrid tears will fall
In death's triumph you leave a broken heart.

You are present in each task that I do
The mind's eye reflects your nearness everywhere
Swamped in grief I seek a way to be with you
Your spirit scorns at thoughts which my mind bears.

Do you recall sweet times of joyous youth
Your wit would outdo the wisdom of Solomon
The tales you told were virtuous with truth
Alas you are gone brave heart, my lover sleep on.

If time is the healer of an open wound
My heart bleeds in vain I shall mend too soon.

Barbara Tunstall

FROM THE SEA

From the sea they gazed with envious eyes
Tempted by cravings they all must pursue
They dreamt of a life 'neath heavenly skies
Dreaming a vision that one day comes true

From the depths of oceans from its abyss
They gathered for an unconscious farewell
And they can but glimpse their preordained bliss
Of a moment where tomorrow does dwell

Fate is the seed evolution must sow
The flower of a future memory
From this simple choice a story will grow
To fulfil the sweet call of destiny.

Leaving their primeval past in the sand
They crawled from the sea to covet the land.

David Bridgewater

WINTER SONNET

Why did Jack Frost steal the day
When winter was but a distant slave
Winter, winter, why have your way
Where nature was spreading, that God gave

Where the trees stood, so bold and bare
When the mist shadows over such beauty
When once those dreams, we did share
As the chilling winds spoil it, so deeply

But still, spring's breath will soon be here
When daffodils show their golden faces
The songs of the birds will bring their cheer
Chirping their different phrase and praises

God bless the day, that the spring brings
Even through winter, as the robin sings

Jean McGovern

THIS COULD BE YOU

As I looked around my garden,
Many weeds did I see,
What! Wild flowers, I beg your pardon,
They look like weeds to me.

My knowledge of plants needs tuning,
And this my good friend knew,
But when the trees and shrubs need pruning,
Of tips I have had a few.

Now the lawns, they are different,
As anyone can see,
Much time on them has been spent,
And all of it by me.

But borders and lawn must go hand in hand,
Then, the future will be as planned.

Will A Tilyard

SONNET

(To Alf)

Yes, there is a darkness on your eyes, my friend,
You cannot see and we just say 'He's blind!'
Yet if we only thought, we'd surely bend
Our heads in shame - for very soon we'd find
We mean ourselves. Truly we live and look
But never fully comprehend nor see
With conscious thankful eyes, sky, trees or book,
Nor yet the tides of the majestic sea.
You do not need the sight of earthly eyes
To know the presence of our God with you:
You find Him in a voice, a hymn, the cries
Of children, poems, songs - in all you do.
Yes, there is darkness on your eyes this night;
But in your soul there shines perpetual light.

Felicity Plumbley

OH HUSH!

Oh hush! What right have you to cry,
To wail that wealth has passed you by?
While you've a roof above your head,
While you can buy your daily bread,
While you have friends? Ah, tell me why.

While you have sight to see the sky
And ears to hear the birds' reply,
Each unto each, as though they said,
'Oh hush! What right to cry?'

When verdant fields before you lie,
When myriad blooms our gardens dye,
When seasons weave a magic thread,
When seeming death brings life instead,
When joy is born and sorrows fly -
Oh hush! No right to cry.

Kathleen M Hatton

THE CONTRACT

Are you certain, have you checked?
The cards against you could be decked.
A devil's hand in sweet disguise,
Could cheat the way your future lies.
Your plans would change and all be wrecked.

The slightest sign that you detect,
Of something wrong and you suspect,
Investigate the hows and whys,
Be certain that you've checked.

No reason why not to inspect
The bottom line and small print text,
For hidden snags and costs that rise,
To hesitate is always wise.
Before you sign the deal perfect.
Are you certain, have you checked?

Pauline Boncey

WHERE IN THE WORLD

Where in the world can once be found
A heart with love deep and profound?
Which he alone with caring gave;
While in his mind mankind to save
On that of blessed hallowed ground.

Now in our hearts does grace abound
While heaven's joys, our lives surround?
Repentant soul no more a knave,
        Where in the world?

O Lord your great quest we propound
To all who wish to hear that sound,
Of freedom's trumpet o'er the grave
Of that which once did but enslave.
And wonder of each brow that frowned!
        Where in the world?

Len Fox

WORDSWORTH - YOU CAN KEEP HIM!

I know what to do - a sonnet I'll write,
Easy! With pen and paper I'm all set,
Inspiration! A subject is simple to get,
So I sit composed and try with all my might,
But I don't think that I will ever get it right,
Wordsworth didn't struggle, I am willing to bet,
Frustration, annoyance - I am starting to sweat,
I will finish this sonnet if it takes me all night.

A published poet is obviously not what I'll be,
I start these things but never seem to have any luck,
Break time. Have a biscuit and a refreshing cup of tea,
These cookies look like they would be easy to cook,
A serial hobbyist is what my hubby calls me,
Now where is that damn recipe book?

Donna M Holt

I WILL SHOW YOU LIFE

Follow me and I will show you life
the very essence, the hidden gem,
the laying down of folly and of strife,
the healing of the hand on hem.

Look to me away from worldly things,
the daily race, the clattering rush,
the place where is the stir of angels' wings,
where deep within is known the silent hush.

Reach out and I will lift you high
far, far above the roar of mighty flood,
for I have heard your longing, ardent cry
and will take you to the very courts of God.

Come, do not hesitate, recoil or fear
the presence of the Son of God is here.

Pamela J Rolinson

EDGE OF THOUGHT

The soul screams out for relief
From the lack of faith in ability
Sunny days can give some though brief
Ready to face the next big calamity

With only the treadmill of daily routine
Negative thoughts deaden the senses
To be feeling so lost is nearly obscene
Crying or cursing puts up defences

Work like automation without rejecting
Willpower and hope that defy explanation
Dismiss the Phantom Enemy as your thinking
Small pleasures that exceed expectation

That inward smile of pleasant thought
Is priceless and can't be bought

Jennifer A Major

SWEET SORROW

This pain of love I'd give away
All chapters of such energy lost
In jealous script and roundelay
Of passions on the tempest tossed

The red of eye and red of ire
Drowning in the silent scream
Unspoken word and fettered thought
Creating tense and stifled dream

But how can lovers' hearts be still
When thoughts unknown drift through their mind?
An empty ache two arms to fill
Unbeckoned fear is all I find

And yet if I'd avoid disgrace
I'd lose the love within your face

Britt Livingstone Fairclough

A CORNISH CHURCH

It stands foursquare against the Cornish sky;
A place of peace and calm where love is found.
A place of worship where the faithful lie
At rest, forever, in the Celtic ground.
In years gone by the faithful came to praise,
On summer mornings and in winters cold.
No cars to bring them, they trod well worn ways;
While in the distance roared the sea to mould
The stones which once showed founding saints the way
To consecrate this place to praise the Lord.
To build their church to last through man's decay
A further thousand years in sweet accord.
Still pilgrims come, of every creed and race;
They kneel in prayer to ask for God's good grace.

Anne James

INTERPRETING THE GENEVA CONVENTION

The view through the bars showed alien trees.
'Help' etc he cried to the indifferent air.
'Won't someone (anyone) answer me please.'
He got off the bed and kicked the chair

Then remembered his captors could see him
through the two-way mirror set in the wall.
'You've really done it this time, Jim,
I don't recognise this place at all.'

The door swung open; two men came in.
'Just a few questions then you can leave.
We'll wire you up then we'll begin.'
'Name, rank and number, that's all I know.'

They left after teaching the meaning of pain.
'Turn that light out' he shouted in vain.

Brian Docherty

LIFE

When I look back upon my life, I find
I can't believe so many years have fled.
So much time musing, dreaming in my mind,
so many great ideas still in my head.
Get up! I tell myself, go out and do
the things you should have done in years gone by;
time will not wait for me, nor yet for you,
succeed or fail, at least I have to try.
Some things are not so easy as before;
the mind is willing, but the legs won't play
experience may 'justredress the score
and I may yet break even on the day.

When I look forward to my life, it seems
the things I've done exceeded all my dreams.

Roger Brougham

EWM - A Vulnerable Minority?

For reasons which our forebears understood,
If we do not, our 'Sceptred Isle' was made
The home for every race and creed and blood,
'Till our identity was lost in shade.
Then, women of our 'green and pleasant land',
Unjustly treated, set their cap to mend
The law; but pressing on, will countermand
Good sense till they must alienate their friends.
And now the British Isles, alas, is dead,
Integrity has vanished with the land.
Let Scotland, Wales and Ireland have their head,
Alone, proud England values where she stands.

Beleaguered though we are, may no man quail
To take his stance as 'English, White and Male!'

John M Beazley

READING

One can lose oneself in reading
As the pages they unfold
Finding there's a lot that's so pleasing
In the stories that are told

Reading is a way for relaxing
It also stimulates the brain
Making for a life less taxing
With the knowledge that you gain

Let your life be filled with knowledge
There is much that you can learn
Even if you've been to college
There is much more to discern

If you need a different outlook
You might find it from a book

Elizabeth Mary Dowler

RED SHOES, GREEN SHIRT

Assorted colours clash within our minds
Angry spirits and restless souls, be still.
True complement, ideal perfection finds
And harmony accords constant goodwill.

This greed to buy, be bought, it matters nought.
The grasping need for diamonds, silver, gold
Or fortunes, riches, rubies, profits sought
Will bring forth cheerless, lonely, darkening cold:

All married themes emerge sweetly combined
With warm caress or tender, gentle kiss.
Where heart is steadfast, good, faithful and kind
There lies serenity and tranquil bliss.

Give me my peace, my calm: no ill, no hurt.
My haven with red shoes and loved green shirt.

Jill Thompson Barker

THE WONDER OF WORDS

Opening my book touching each page
What would her story hold
Will pages excite as mysteries unfold
Through tranquil summer's day I shall laze
Turning crisp leaves revealing epic maze
Of damsels in distress hunky heroes bold
Captivated words as each characters rolled
Clusters of print bringing make-believe haze
An imaginary plot takes over our minds
The souls of characters begin to reveal
Between fresh pages with soft leather binds
As author scribes his pen mightier than steel
Taking us on epic journey that twist and turns
Towards the epilogue of this story so real

Ann Hathaway

CARELESS INTENT

In the days of my very early youth,
Courtesy was shown and given freely,
But now it seems that one can be uncouth,
And show contempt by bicycle wheelie.

In the main street or road of any town,
The youth parade showing no fear or thought,
Hoping to be top dog and wear the crown,
Unconcerned with the very danger brought.

Which may just maim or cause an accident,
To themselves and others of whom may be,
Unaware of their nature of intent,
Just for them to show off to you and me.

One day these very hell-bent youths will know,
Careless acts kill, rather than make a show.

Nigel Lloyd Maltby

SPORTS FAN

O dark-miened mistress of your netball team,
O graceful, golden goddess of the courts
Your eyes reflect like stars your girls' esteem
As you hold sway, disposing netball thoughts.

Young wands of will reach forth to catch your spark
As you implant your lore in questing minds.
Tough macho master of the soccer park
I too, am 'thralled by your swart spell that binds.

Not for my lads who failed to notch their scores
But for your girls who failed to clinch their game
- I'd constant lose, could victory be yours -
I'd gladly, oh! so gladly take the blame.

O let me plaster o'er your girls' scraped knees
And slice your half-time oranges, Miss, please . . .

Frederick Poole

EASTER IS HERE

Easter is here be it so late,
We will meet at the pearly gate,
There to rejoice a light on high,
Go from Earth without a goodbye,
Suddenly you have made a date.

Who knows what is to be your fate?
On this journey do not be late,
Angels will take you through the sky,
Easter is here.

Accidents happen do not wait,
The worry caused does not abate,
There is no time to tell a lie,
Not even time to say goodbye,
You will be flying at this rate,
Easter is here.

M Lawson

WE CHASE THE RAINBOW

We chase the rainbow steadfastly,
Hoping a crock of gold we will see.
It is a fact we suffer the strain,
In striving for what money can attain.
Why do we count such misery?

The fetters we forge won't set us free,
They make slaves of us in constancy.
As we relentlessly search for gain,
               We chase the rainbow.

A lack of wealth brings forth many sighs,
Can't we see what's before our eyes?
Disenchantment brings grief and pain,
As hopes for riches still remain,
               We chase the rainbow.

M Wakefield

LOWRY STREET

Lowry street stands great and crowded
Under awnings men are shrouded
Busily the women do shop
Going past fashion shops they stop
Clothes and hats make them astounded

Squashed up stores the sky unclouded
Through some doors much music sounded
As pigeons roost on the roof top
                    Lowry street stands.

People talked, some people shouted
Where to shop, some people doubted
Place to place advertisers hop
Selling vacuum cleaner and mop
Roofs all flat, pointy or rounded
                    Lowry street stands.

Christopher Johnson (12)

ETERNAL SPRING

Eternal spring in all we see
With flowers that attract the bee.
And swallows come back home to nest
When at the early sun's behest
Birds' sweet dawn chorus soothes our rest.

The yellow of the primrose bright
The bluebells makes a wondrous sight
High up in a tree a robin sings
                          Eternal spring.

Sun shines to chase the dew at morn
Like teardrops on the rose at dawn
Lambs skip and play around the fields
Man sows and prays for fruitful yields
Sun dips behind the mountain's rim
                          Eternal spring.

Doreen E Todd

MY LITTLE BLACK DRESS

It's just too tight, I hear the cry,
Could I adjust or rectify.
Optimistic, I was so sure
It fitted well the time before.
A weight gain 'my dress' does imply.

No more eating to satisfy,
On healthy food I would rely.
Excited then - until I saw,
It's just too tight.

It doesn't matter what I try
Too late, nothing can beautify
My figure, I chose to ignore
Hoping one day, I would restore
My dress size 'but' I heave a sigh,
It's just too tight.

Beverley Diana Burcham

WE LIVE IN HOPE

We live in hope that peace shall reign.
An end to war and battles vain -
Nations rave when lives are taken;
Families mourn, their faith is shaken,
Homes reduced to charred remains.

When life is hell and filled with pain,
Can they survive and yet be sane?
If there is light when they awaken,
We live in hope.

Oh wretched war to those a bane,
Grant them the strength to rise again.
Lest they should fail we now will hasten
To those who think they are forsaken;
The world must change for some 'tis plain.
We live in hope.

Ann Madge

CORPOREAL CHARACTERISTICS

As part of mankind we experience some imperfection,
Map out our lives no matter in what direction.
The choice is ours, integrity or crime,
Select paths in life all throughout our time,
Faultless in life with no infection.

Throughout our lives we require constant correction,
To bring about love, compassion and perfection,
Postulation may be the norm, dismissing all grime,
As part of mankind.

Serious are many people with a fixed expression,
With many people displaying parental aggression.
We encounter many acts in life, starting from birth,
All we hope with no reflection,
As part of mankind.

John P Evans

THE PRICE WE PAY

The price we pay at times is high
When late in life we wonder why
We ignored things we had been told
And went through life on stony roads
How often do we hear that sigh

Lost time is never there to buy
The chance is gone when time goes by
We pay more now for what we hold
The price we pay at times is high

When dreams are just pies in the sky
We make the beds on which we lie
And learn too late when we are old
All things that glitter are not gold
And lacking that discerning eye
The price we pay at times is high

K W Benoy

PERSEPHONE PERSONIFIED

'Tis age which maketh me so sad
I think on death, perchance, as good or bad
I recall what Frances' dying words were
Where has my beauty gone, where to inter
But do these thoughts make me mad?

'Tis age which maketh me not glad
As if youth's follies were a passing fad
This weariness of hours: what infer?
    Which maketh me so sad.

I scree deep like mist through Scottish plaid
Shadows of my youth, they were trifles, a mere tad
To the brooding clay I will deter
But goddess gay, sometimes, winter's Demeter:
Like progeny of ashes: lass and lad -
    Which maketh me so sad.

Joy Sheridan

As Spring Blossom

As spring blossom floats far away
On breezes born of yesterday,
We cup our hands to catch what's gone
And wonder why there's always none.
What need we do to stop it stray?

The sun delights our hearts by day.
The night brings fear to which we're prey.
We feel as fragile and alone
As spring blossom.

Yet when we realise, and we may,
We are the rhythm of life's way;
That life and moments are as one
And harmonise in actions done,
That breath and life is interplay:
Then we blossom.

Lorenza Cangiano

THE BEST MAN WON

The bells ring out for me, my friend,
you spurned your love and would not mend
the broken heart you threw away.
So, now we have this wedding day,
and all because you would not bend.

A willing ear you would not lend.
When I did see the courtship end
you said you wouldn't beg and pray.
The bells ring out.

Your lady love I did befriend.
To her a sweet bouquet did send.
So clear and straight the pathway lay
towards this wondrous wedding day.
Your actions you cannot defend.
The bells ring out.

Delia Shaw

A RONDEAU FOR CHRISTOPHER COLUMBUS

Columbus discovered the US of A,
His ship pointed west and he set off one day,
The Earth was thought flat like a path or a ledge,
If one sailed too far, one would fall off the edge,
One man didn't think it was really that way.

The intrepid explorer just wanted his say,
He felt that land beyond the horizon lay,
Columbus.

He thought Earth was shaped in a spherical way,
He felt if he sailed west, he'd make India one day,
He needed some ships and provisions and crew,
So he went to the palace and made a to-do,
And persuaded the king to finance his foray,
Columbus.

Intrepid explorer, Christopher Columbus, set out not knowing
Where he was going, arrived not knowing where we was,
and returned not knowing where he had been.

Mick Nash

Singing

I understand now the God you know so well,
Peter, and delight in the skilful way you tell
us what you mean in the poems you made.
Your words carefully chosen, an arcade
of interwoven ideas, a groundswell

of meaning, a shining reverberating bell
singing loud and clear, no soft sell
here, yet I cannot dig with your spade
I understand now.

Your lifelong journey down dale, up fell
a quest for treasure, to motivate not quell
my own search. I rest in the shade
seeing your light shining, a little less afraid
of instinct, yet not ready to trust in the spell
I understand now.

Ann Westgarth

ONE DAY I SAID

One day I said that I loved you,
Then you said that you loved me too.
By ties of love together bound,
Mum and daughter united I found.
Now how will I cope without you?

Sudden death, then what should I do,
I'm left feeling empty and blue.
Cried rivers, but not making sounds,
One day I said . . .

Remember trips'to local zoo,
Asking questions: How, what or who?
Although always portly and round,
Value for laughter with each pound.
But then up to heaven you flew,
One day I said . . .

S Mullinger

TRAPPED BENEATH POISONED LIGHT

The sun poisons this humdrum disgrace,
It sparkles, shines and illuminates,
All I see is the descent of Beelzebub's face.

Life's enigmatic evolution, one can easily grace,
As constant waste has took its toll,
The sun poisons this humdrum disgrace.

My weary eyes hold lost love to trace,
But I'm imprisoned by guilt and everlasting shame,
All I see is the descent of Beelzebub's face.

Creepy guttersnipes plague this grim place,
Interlopers lurk as ignorance is blatant.
The sun poisons this humdrum disgrace.

I picture a town full of pure lace,
But we're all primitive carnivores,
All I see is the descent of Beelzebub's face.

We've never walked at the same pace.
Hail the dawning of invincible unity,
The sun poisons this humdrum disgrace.
All I see is the descent of Beelzebub's face.

Simon Cardy

EILEEN

I named my miracle Eileen,
Saw you through a misted glow.
Angelic, soft, pristine.

Heaven blessed me with a queen,
Graced me with your love and so,
I named my miracle Eileen.

Loving, loved, gentle, serene,
Through life may you ever go,
Angelic, soft, pristine.

Such precious gift has never been,
So let man and heaven know,
I named my miracle Eileen.

Across your dainty cot I lean,
Touch the wonder there below,
Angelic, soft, pristine.

I dream your future yet unseen,
Hear my heartbeat whisper low,
I named my miracle Eileen,
Angelic, soft, pristine.

Tony Coyle

ZIMMER RACE

Granny went in a zimmer race
We backed her through thick or thin
But she ended up in second place.

She did up her wrinkled face,
Practised with a wheelie bin,
Granny went in a zimmer race.

Granny stopped to tie her lace
She straightened up with a grin,
But she ended up in second place.

At dinner Granny took her place
Planned tactics with a baked beans tin.
Granny went in a zimmer race.

She set off at a great pace,
Thought that she was sure to win,
But she ended up in second place.

Granny took part with great grace,
To lose she'd take it on the chin.
Granny went in a zimmer race
But she ended up in second place.

Frank Keetley

So Sad

So sad is me up in this tree,
I have no one to twitter to.
Life is boring as can be.

I'm lonely I need company,
Feathers brown but I feel blue.
So sad is me up in this tree.

No one else will play with me,
I don't look the way they do.
Life is boring as can be.

Someone dumped me, then did flee,
I'm scared of heights, don't like the view.
So sad is me up in this tree.

I can't get down, I need my tea,
Up here there's only bugs to chew.
Life is as boring as can be.

I'll call for help and make my plea,
'Please, cock-a-doodle-doo!'
So sad is me up in this tree.
Life is boring as can be.

Karen Brooke

DON'T ENQUIRE

'Tis not for us to know our fate;
What life may have for us in store.
'Tis not a subject for debate.

Some over crystal balls will prate.
Their forecasts we must all ignore.
'Tis not for us to know our fate.

Of 'reading' hands, one has to state,
(And here these words I must outpour,)
'Tis not for us to know our fate.

Tell those who would presume to state
That they can see beyond death's door,
'Tis not a subject for debate.

There are those who would postulate
That what's to come we've seen before.
'Tis not for us to know our fate:
'Tis not a subject for debate.

Eric W Baker

VILLANELLE

My love has gone away from me:
He isn't there for me to see.
We no longer speak or look or touch.

Back to work with the gloom,
The sun won't shine on me again,
My love has gone away from me.

We look today and look tomorrow.
Keeping faith, hope and love
We no longer speak or look or touch.

My tears come often,
The ache is in my heart.
My love has gone away from me.

We felt at ease and laughed and laughed.
We cared and could do no wrong.
We no longer, speak or look or touch.

Sadly we parted and said goodbye.
Time heals, love never dies.
My love has gone away from me,
We no longer speak or look or touch.

Rita Jane Williams

LOVE'S UNITY

Happy are those who coincide:
Who live as one and yet as parts.
Who neither clash nor yet collide.

The lover mingled with his bride,
A harmony of loving hearts.
Happy are those who coincide.

Together moving with the tide
Of shifting time omniscience charts:
Who neither clash nor yet collide.

Their love forever ocean wide,
One vision held which grace imparts.
Happy are those who coincide.

Their lives display a humbled pride,
Where cherished self in death departs.
Who neither clash nor yet collide.

No wars, all feuding set aside:
Free to pursue the gentler arts.
Happy are those who coincide,
Who neither clash nor yet collide.

Paul Brittain

GENE LINES

'I have arrived,' I heard your strident cry
raucous in birth, a tempest as a gift
with love quite fierce enough to terrify.

Each eager day brought smiles to satisfy
our storm of love, to give our hearts a lift.
'I have arrived,' I heard your strident cry.

You cut teeth, we gritted ours, no lullaby
shortening the bleak cold night's long drift,
with love quite fierce enough to terrify.

Then as the sly deceitful years fled by
we reached that tortured time of teenage rift:
'I have arrived,' I heard your strident cry.

And you reached out beyond our grasp to try
your arm against the world, as blood ran swift
with love quite fierce enough to terrify.

So to new birth, with love to sanctify
this raucous life, while I felt eras shift.
'I have arrived,' I heard that strident cry
with love quite fierce enough to terrify.

John Statham

MY HEART FLOATS ON A LAKE OF PAIN

My heart floats on a lake of pain:
The boat is gone, the boat was you.
Who else but myself can I blame?

The sun has given way to rain;
Black horizon comes into view.
My heart floats on a lake of pain.

Gullible is my middle name;
Easy for me to misconstrue.
Who else but myself can I blame?

You treated my love with disdain:
What misery you put me through.
My heart floats on a lake of pain.

Your arrogant love had no shame;
Each promise proved to be untrue.
Who else but myself can I blame?

I vow I'll not be hurt again,
If it's the last thing that I do.
My heart floats on a lake of pain.
Who else but myself can I blame?

Pauline Ilsley

SPIRIT OF AFRICA

Shadow of the mist, grey Goliath embraces dawn's breaking light
drab leathered skin dominating, unyielding giant of ancient years
shimmering figure of legend, ivory illusion tusks faded white

empowered with awesome strength, burning energy of muscled might
Africa's ethereal spirit, piercing the veil of trickled tears
shadow of the mist, grey Goliath embraces dawn's breaking light

feeding vitality's force, spiritual shadow standing, potent power bright
haunting spectral shade, vapour of the mind,
provoking flap of wrinkled ears
shimmering figure of legend, ivory illusion tusks faded white

trumpeting echo of Titan's trunk, disturbs peaceful breath in flight
outline mingled with enveloping gloom, courts obscuring haze of
whispered fears
shadow of the mist, grey Goliath embraces dawn's breaking light

eager cloak of secrecy drawing tight, immersed in jungle depths black
as night
stout silhouettes illuminated, dancing lightning's lance,
booming thunder nears
shimmering figure of legend, ivory illusion tusks faded white

granite beast unbroken, dampened denizen resists the storm at its height
lumbering tusker caressed by stealthy sun, darkened clouds of doom
slowly clear
shadow of the mist, grey Goliath embraces dawn's breaking light
shimmering figure of legend, ivory illusion tusks faded white

Chris Bailey

SILENT CHIME

Long muted dancer, imprisoned, dim-lit dungeon your crumbling shell
desolate bastion of wounded faith, between dwarfing oak
head bowed you kneel
tenacious dust of solitude, embraces silent chime of dormant bell

abandoned in apathy, into dark desolate days of disrepair you fell
swirling leaves and wind-blown litter invade your haven,
breaking barren seal
long muted dancer, imprisoned, dim-lit dungeon your crumbling shell

stone intruder nestled in leaf-clad shadows, humble in the tree lined dell
hushed house of worship softly sleeping,
time for ancient wounds to heal
tenacious dust of solitude, embraces silent chime of dormant bell

stifled sound whispers about creaking beams,
craving joy of songful swell
melodious ghosts of ages past echo fellowship,
with spirits of unsounded zeal
long muted dancer, imprisoned, dim-lit dungeon your crumbling shell

peaceful flight of wings disturbed, circle redundant
tower with tales to tell
providing shelter within creeping coma of rumbling ruin,
murmuring life to feel
tenacious dust of solitude, embraces silent chime of dormant bell

muffled moments tread tranquil calm, easing your empty stagnant hell
wandering witness to eroding elements, stealthily surrounding,
final breath to steal
long muted dancer, imprisoned, dim-lit dungeon your crumbling shell
tenacious dust of solitude, embraces silent chime of dormant bell

Paul Birkitt

FIDELITY PERSONIFIED

It comforts me to see your faithful eyes
And look of pure devotion on your face,
Such perfect love, incapable of lies.

Though others may be daunted by your size
You complement my life with poise and grace;
It comforts me to see your faithful eyes.

You listen without judgement or surprise;
A picture of integrity and faith,
Such perfect love, incapable of lies.

To guard my life you'd never compromise,
I know you'd do your best to keep me safe,
It comforts me to see your faithful eyes.

We share a bond of love that never dies,
Much undervalued by the human race,
Such perfect love, incapable of lies.

Oh little wolf I love your barks and cries,
Your gentle licks and genuine embrace;
It comforts me to see your faithful eyes,
Such perfect love, incapable of lies.

J M Redfern-Hayes

R.I.P

Beneath this grey cold granite stone,
In memory, seek me not here.
It is not for me a home.

I am rested now and all but bone.
In body, pain will not sear.
Beneath this cold grey granite stone.

My spirit risen and not alone.
Death no longer for me holds its fear.
It is not for me a home.

The trees, the flowers are where I roam.
For earthly sorrows I neither care.
Beneath this cold grey granite stone.

I now await for your time to come.
So weep no longer any tear.
It is not for me a home.

In memory, I will be to some,
As among the clouds I soar.
For beneath this cold grey granite stone,
It is not for me a home.

Peter Coakley

MISSING YOU

I miss you more than words can say.
I think about you all the time.
I long for you in every way.

I wish you would come back to stay.
Without you, life's not worth a dime.
I miss you more than words can say.

The clouds are dark, the sky is grey.
Amid the dust and dirt and grime,
I long for you in every way.

You will return, I hope, I pray.
For us to part would seem a crime.
I miss you more than words can say.

For me, there is no night and day.
For me, the bells no longer chime.
I long for you in every way.

There is no price I would not pay;
No mountain that I would not climb.
I miss you more than words can say.
I long for you in every way.

James Williams

GET A LIFE

Fulfil a wish and savour the memory -
Don't let opportunities go to waste,
Or your scrapbook of life will stay empty.

There are so many things to do and see;
All those opportunities to be faced -
Fulfil a wish and savour the memory.

You owe it to yourself to be happy:
From life's banquet find new flavours to taste
Or your scrapbook of life will stay empty.

Make your world into a thrilling story
That would be read in excited haste:
Fulfil a wish and savour the memory.

Grasp ambition; be who you want to be,
Discover some adventures to be chased
Or your scrapbook of life will stay empty.

Seize for yourself handfuls of life's glory,
Turn fears into challenges to be faced;
Fulfil a wish and savour the memory
Or your scrapbook of life will stay empty.

Kim Latham

MY LOVE

Where will I find my love to be?
I fain would seek by night and day
A champion ever true to me.

How will I know he is fancy free
And ready to glance my way?
Where will I find my love to be?

I pray that someone hears my plea
And when I find him he will stay
A champion ever true to me.

Is there a paragon such as he
For me to cherish and obey?
Where will I find my love to be?

I challenge the whole world to see
My honour that could not betray
A champion ever true to me.

At dusk I dream beneath a tree
Of orange blossom in early May.
Where will I find my love to be?
A champion ever true to me.

Tessa Dewhurst

A Different World

A different world I've seen,
It's so beautiful to see,
It's breathtaking like a dream.

To this stunning world I've been,
Then open my eyes to see,
A different world I've seen.

I walk and talk with Daphine,
Taking in all that's to see,
It's breathtaking like a dream.

I adore to sit and beam
At this gorgeous thing to me
A different world I've seen.

Of this world I'm very keen,
I'm pleased that it's all to me,
It's breathtaking like a dream.

Though sometimes I sit and dream,
Of some day having company,
A different world I've seen,
It's breathtaking like a dream.

S *Julie Hobbs*

BLUE IS MY ROSE

My garden rose has failed to bloom
Sadness sets a tear in my eye
Rose growers' pellets adorn my garden room.

I hope this rose will perform very soon
Shortly I expect to see a coating of blackfly
My garden rose has failed to bloom.

Disappointment in my rose named after a tune
I keep asking myself the reason why
Rose growers' pellets adorn my garden room.

I must make sure not to fume
Harder next time I must try
My garden rose has failed to bloom.

Should I contact an expert or two
Perhaps I could sing its song to the sky
Rose growers' pellets adorn my garden room.

Will I ever see your beauty my rose Blue Moon
O dear, O dear where does the problem lie?
My garden rose has failed to bloom
Rose growers' pellets adorn my garden room.

Roger Foster

YVONNE

This was how I met Yvonne,
Standing near her maisonette,
In a gown of gay cretonne.

She wore shoes with buckles on
And her hair was flowing jet,
This was how I met Yvonne.

Then I said, 'My name is John,'
Toying with my epaulette
This was how I met Yvonne.

She was grand to look upon,
Playing with a small rosette,
In a gown of gay cretonne.

All desire to smoke had gone,
I put out my cigarette,
This was how I met Yvonne,
In a gown of gay cretonne.

Sarah Hunter

THE TREE OF DESTINY

Upright it stood, in the midst of despair,
Resisting the force of a flood severe.
It was destined to be a cradle there.

A tree, full of life, provided care
For a stricken family full of fear:
Upright it stood in the midst of despair.

In former times, when life was fair,
Many a nestling it helped to rear:
It was destined to be a cradle there.

The fruit of life it was soon to bear:
A pregnant mother's time was near,
Upright it stood in the midst of despair.

Born was the child in surroundings rare:
A limb of the tree held the baby dear.
It was destined to be a cradle there.

Our world rejoiced when made aware
A mighty tree gave cause to cheer;
Upright it stood in the midst of despair;
It was destined to be a cradle there.

Margaret Knox Stubbs

PRIMROSE AND PINK CAMPION

Near where the millwheel threshes on,
Our April eyes together saw
Pale primrose and pink campion.

All possible, our plight upon
The bridge above the churn and flow
Just where the millwheel threshes on.

And we were infinite and one
And ringed according to the law
Of primrose and pink campion.

Of silver in the sunstruck swan,
Beside the chaff of droplets' glow
Near where the millwheel threshes on.

Do you recall our strange temptation
To plunge into the black below
The primrose and pink campion,

Knowing I would walk alone
(You distant where I cannot follow)
Near where the millwheel threshes on,
The primrose and pink campion?

John McPartlin

I'VE BEEN CHANGED

Jesus Your power has changed me,
My love for You will grow and grow,
Knowing You has set me free.

I never know what the pathway will be,
But Your guiding light will the way show,
Jesus Your power has changed me.

Every day You give me new treasures to see,
Gifts from You, in my heart, I know,
Knowing You has set me free.

Growth flourishes in me like new buds on a tree,
Blessings unto me Lord You bestow,
Jesus Your power has changed me.

Doubt, pain and sorrow away from me did flee,
Also away with all things making me feel low,
Knowing You has set me free.

To dear Lord I pray on bended knee,
Your power fills me constantly with a warm glow
Jesus Your power has changed me
Knowing You has set me free.

Chris Jackson

MOUNTAIN WORSHIP

Mountains plunging downward to the sea,
Houses crowded near the shore, between,
Magic of the scene seduces me.

At every turn a new discovery,
From sandy beach to deepest dark ravine,
Mountains plunging downward to the sea.

Three famous peaks in glorious dignity,
A master sculptor worked with hand unseen,
Magic of the scene seduces me.

Sunset on this brilliant panoply,
Red ball, black boulders, everywhere serene,
Mountains plunging downward to the sea.

Mountain lover I, a hill-hippy,
Bedazzled by the vista, by the sheen,
Magic of the scene seduces me.

What upheaval in the earth's geology
Caused these unique shapes to convene!
Mountains plunging downward to the sea,
Magic of the scene seduces me.

Rachel Silbert

PROFIT AND LOSS

Old Charlie really loved a juicy thick pork chop,
Rising slowly, his first daily task was always the same,
Too old in tooth his wily ways he could not stop.

Off he plodded beside busy roads, to find the butcher's shop,
His body not so agile now, for he had a leg quite lame.
Old Charlie really loved a juicy thick pork chop.

To rest a while onto the pavement he sometimes had to flop,
With ageing bones his survival was no playful game.
Too old in tooth his wily ways he could not stop.

On his way no cooling shade, overhead the sun so hot,
Hunger pangs so sharp, would his quest be in vain?
Old Charlie really loved a juicy thick pork chop.

Nose twitching at succulent aroma, he saw meat on table drop.
Reflected in butcher's window, stealthily round the wall he came,
Too old in tooth his wily ways he could not stop.

Nearing the table, aches forgotten, he jumped and grabbed the lot,
Safe in the alley, tucking in, butcher's loss, Charlie's gain.
Old Charlie really loved a juicy thick pork chop,
Too old in tooth his wily ways he could not stop.

Wendy Newton

EATING NAPKINS

I am the rebel with a cause,
I rip this flesh in my jaws,
I use injustice to wipe my floors,
I'll take my revenge without a pause

For breath, which slowly nags and knaws
I'm rubbing my household sores
I am the murderer, with this knife,
I'll suffer as I am the rebel, I rebel.

I don't stalk the bloodstained walls,
I'll walk, itching; those foreign wars,
Famine ringing the kitchen, rife,
Inject the poison, it burns alive,
Digest this calling with all my flaws,
I am the rebel. I remain. I rebel.

Harry Carver

A NEW LOVE

She stood at a Soho bar in a corduroy suit
with long black tresses on route
to nowhere fast, drunk on the grape
of France, liquorice eyes (yum! yum!) wide agape.
While I, a maker of paths, transformed from newt
to princely frog thought her dead cute:
Heard in my honeyed head a symphonic suite
on a stave like a chocolate buttoned gate.
Out of burnt ashes love's phoenix formed.

What corduroy fate had handed me I took. A flute
I heard with strings playing a motif en route
to a brassy dance on a path for lovers - a state
of momentary bliss - a country estate
of roses and blackbirds with gold thread suits.
Out of burnt ashes love's phoenix stormed.

Evan Gwyn Williams

FLOWERS OF THE HEART

The memories in my heart so gently pressed
Like everlasting flowers to never fade.
Reminding how sweet life was ever blessed
With love and joy since wedding vows were made.

The sweet flowers of each kiss and warm embrace,
Of tender moments veiled in secrecy.
The flowers of birth that lit a father's face
As lullabies were sung so lovingly.

How sweet the flowers of friendships warming glow:
How fair the flowers of constant faithfulness;
A lovely place in solitude to go,
This rainbow garden of great joyfulness.

Then spring the flowers of loneliness and sighs
Since time came love to say our last goodbyes.

Violet Corlett

THOUGHTS OF SUMMER

Hurrah! Summer's coming, what a delight
To see the sun and feel a warm breeze.
What a pleasure to have an evening that's light.

The flowers will bloom, what a pretty sight,
And working hard are the busy bees.
Hurrah! Summer's coming, what a delight.

We won't pull the curtains, there's no fire to light.
We won't catch a cold or ever sneeze.
What a pleasure to have an evening that's light.

Birds will be singing, they rest in their flight
To sit in the branches of leaf covered trees.
Hurrah! Summer's coming, what a delight.

Everyone's happy, well no, not quite,
Jack Frost won't be able to do his big freeze.
What a pleasure to have an evening that's light.

To get up in the morning with a sky so bright.
Don't lay in bed, no excuses please!
Hurrah! Summer's coming, what a delight,
What a pleasure to have an evening that's light.

Gladys Baillie

PLEASURE

I like to look around me
To make pictures at my leisure
Oh the lovely things I see.

Through my window the great oak tree
Always gives me pleasure
I like to look around me.

Birds fly down and then they flee
In springtime without measure
Oh the lovely things I see.

Sheep grazing o'er green hill and valley
Graceful swans on the river
I like to look around me.

White cliffs sweeping down to blue sea
The boats with sails aquiver
Oh the lovely things I see.

For a paintbrush I must plea
To keep these scenes for ever
I like to look around me
Oh the lovely things I see.

Barbara Fosh

WILL WE RETURN?

Will we come back, will we return again,
To that nostalgic land of honeydew
The land where there is never any pain,

You have departed and my life is vain
Morning and night I wait and dream of you
Will we come back, will we return again?

Oh will you be reality again
When I arrive within that realm so true -
The land where there is never any pain.

Love of my heart, let me not long in vain
Once more in that strange land to be with you
Will we come back, will we return again?

Oh life so transient and so harsh 'tis plain
We always knew we'd see that land so true
The land where there is never any pain!

In spite of all life's puzzles it is plain
The only question that I ask of you -
Will we come back, will we return again
To land where there is never any pain?

A Goodwin

SECRETS

Today has gone, tomorrow's yet to play
In the darkness of the night,
There are things that I must say.

The deed it must be done
Whispering softly in your ear,
Today is gone, tomorrow's yet to play.

If there was any other way
My heart aches to tell you this
There are things that I must say.

Now the act is done,
Here is one last kiss,
Today has gone, tomorrow's yet to play.

It is clear you want me to stay
My cheek is wet from tears,
There are things that I must say.

True love is never lost,
We have paid the cost . . .
Today has gone, tomorrow's yet to play,
There are things that I must say.

Jean Griffin

THEY KEPT THE FAITH

They kept the faith; they knew his majesty,
Prophets and Patriarchs illumined night.
They worshipped God for all eternity.

Jesus' disciples, fishers of the sea,
They served their Lord; they saw his vision bright.
They kept the faith; they knew his majesty.

The early Christians entered stumblingly
Into new worlds; their mission to bring light.
They worshipped God for all eternity.

The martyrs of the Church, knowing they would be
Cast into flame, were never put to flight.
They kept the faith; they knew his majesty.

The architects and painters artistry
Raised up our hearts and souls to Heavens height.
They worshipped God for all eternity.

Now we who struggle still to solve the mystery,
Remember those whose lives gave hope and sight.
They kept the faith; they knew his majesty,
They worshipped God for all eternity.

Anne James

VILLANELLE

I think of you at break of day,
Remember you at set of sun.
The hours seem long now you're away.

I knew you could no longer stay.
My *waiting time* has just begun.
I think of you at break of day.

I watch the children as they play
Or gather flowers one by one.
The hours seem long now you're away.

I sit alone. What could I say
When people ask what you have done?
I think of you at break of day.

Throughout the sunny month of May,
Remembering walks and games and fun,
The hours seem long now you're away.

'Come safely home' I always pray.
To welcome you how I shall run!
I think of you at break of day.
The hours seem long now you're away.

Daphne Wilkinson

EBB AND FLOW

While summer gulls in blue skies soar,
There stands a couple, golden tanned;
Waves wild and free crash on the shore.

She cannot bear this anymore,
She hurls his golden wedding band,
While summer gulls in blue skies soar.

His heart is shaken to the core,
To lose her's more than he can stand,
Waves wild and free crash on the shore.

He speaks in words she can't ignore,
He strokes her hair, a single strand,
While summer gulls in blue skies soar.

She listens as the blue waves roar,
He puts the ring into her hand,
Waves wild and free crash on the shore.

She looks at him, their eyes adore,
They trace a love heart in the sand,
While summer gulls in blue skies soar,
Waves wild and free crash on the shore.

Katrina Shepherd

ABORTION?

It is bigger growing.
Forming, becoming like me,
Do I have the heart for a killing?

It is my life, my living,
Do I need extra company?
It is bigger growing.

It is the time to be deciding,
I am thinking constantly,
Do I have the heart for a killing?

Myself it is tearing,
A weight permanently,
It is bigger growing.

I need more time, everlasting,
Oh, what should it be?
Do I have the heart for a killing?

It is time for the deciding,
I am numb, no sensitivity,
It is bigger growing,
Do I have the heart for a killing?

Zoe Puttock

WHEN I LOOK IN MY LOVER'S EYES

When I look in my lover's eyes,
I wonder if he loves just me.
I know not where the true heart lies.

I see the lights of midnight skies,
Pinpoints of stellar brilliancy,
When I look in my lover's eyes.

Sometimes he'll tease and tantalise,
Engaging in duplicity.
I know not where the true heart lies.

Age does not always make us wise
And I feel anxious frequently,
When I look in my lover's eyes.

I've plumbed the lows, I've scaled the highs,
Unsure of his constancy.
I know not where the true heart lies.

At last I've come to realise
That love is what I wish to see
When I look in my lover's eyes.
I know not where the true heart lies.

Celia G Thomas

FROM DARK TO LIGHT

Yellow and white of early spring
Shows among the new green blades
Cancelling out deep winter's sting.

Birds start soaring on the wing,
Celandines soon line the glades,
Yellow and white of early spring.

New early shoots appearing,
People busy with their spades,
Cancelling out deep winter's sting.

Clear chalk streams now hosting
Marigolds of various shades,
Yellow and white of early spring.

The cuckoo soon starts calling
And a song bird serenades,
Cancelling out deep winter's sting.

The warmer days are bringing
Life to nature, men and maids,
Yellow and white of early spring
Cancelling out deep winter's sting.

Kathleen White

CONSTANT IN THE NIGHT

The stars shine bright
They're there for you
Constant in the night.

The stars are there for your delight
Whatever you may do
The stars shine bright.

Beaming down pale light
For whatever takes its cue
Constant in the night.

Nocturnal animals howl and fight
Is that all they do?
The stars shine bright.

From such a great height
Sometimes many, sometimes a few
Constant in the night.

Who created this - what Might!
This splendour, daily anew
The stars shine bright
Constant in the night.

Anna Evelyn

BRING FOLK TO CHRIST THE WHOLE WORLD ROUND

The steeple bell peels out its sound
Footsteps hurry along the street,
Bring folk to Christ the whole world round.

Some pass the door, while others found
Their sanctuary in silent prayer,
The steeple bell peels out its sound.

The verger brings the book renowned
The choir enters full of song,
Bring folk to Christ the whole world round.

The service starts with hymn and round
While prayers upon the air rise up
The steeple bell peels out its sound.

Between the peels the church is crowned
In beauty of a special kind
Bring folk to Christ the whole world round.

The hour has passed, silent to sound,
Some smile, some weep, some look ahead,
The steeple bell peels out its sound,
Bring folk to Christ, the whole world round.

Elizabeth M Sudder

ON THE SQUARE

The Square is almost deserted and still.
From a white tower strange flags fly.
A whistle shrieks from a steam train - eerie and shrill.

Giorgio de Chirico was once mentally ill.
Two giant artichokes grow shadows as they lie.
The Square is almost deserted and still.

Beware the lurking shadows! Someone might kill.
Above all - there's a green and yellow sky.
A whistle shrieks from a steam train - eerie and shrill.

Is it from a reverie - a nightmare - or even a little pill?
Coal-black train, your smoke plume is waving goodbye.
The Square is almost deserted and still.

Time hangs suspended until . . .
De Chirico's weird paintings delight my eye.
A whistle shrieks from a steam train - eerie and shrill.

Picture The Square's imagination, and artistic skill.
If Freud could analyse this - would it be who? What? When? Or why?
The Square is almost deserted and still.
A whistle shrieks from a steam train - eerie and shrill.

Mark Young

FOR YOUR LOVE I'LL

For your love I'll always be there,
Within a dream world that we share.
Where the sea greets a morning dawn,
Like beauty in a unicorn.
A vision of a love so rare.

About the way we came to care,
In a game made for two we dare.
To show our hearts broken and torn,
For your love I'll.

Remove all the pain that you bear.
Then no one, not ever never can tear;
Us apart 'cos we will be born,
Again from all that is forlorn.
When angels from heaven draw near,
For your love I'll.

Amanda Jayne Biro

Up, Up and Away

Up, up and away, are you coming too?
The Saviour is also calling to you
A loud command and trumpet call
And you will see the Lord of all
Yes he is coming into view.

It is not by sitting in a pew
But by true faith a believing few
Cries out, 'Catch us lest we fall'
Up, up and away.

Oh God we pray our lives renew
All our sins we solemnly rue
Not for us a black or purple pall
Or indeed the Wormwood and the gall
Reigning forever O Lord with you
Up, up and away.

Margaret Harrold

TEA DANCE

Sophisticated strains of soft refrain;
Incessant chatter in between each score;
Pulsating chords that captivate the brain
Initiate the urge to take the floor.

The dancing at this hour stands out alone
Expectant warm, exciting, bright, alive,
When band strikes up, it quickly sets the tone
Inviting young relationships to thrive.

Within a trice of afternoon begun
All tensions ease and movement starts to flow.
Enjoyment is in store for everyone
A world away from stressful care and woe.

Unique is music's power to fulfil,
Enrich, enhance, enliven - even thrill!

Jack Conway

THE SUN IN MY LIFE

To me you are just like the golden sun,
You rise much higher in the eastern skies.
You are with me now and when I was young,
And above the nations you always rise.
Without your presence I'd cease to exist,
So it would be wrong of me to pretend.
If you were to go, you'd be greatly missed.
To me and others it would be the end.
Your warmth transmits to every boy and girl -
Although sometimes they take you for granted.
With your shining smile you colour the world,
Which would fail, of course, if you departed.
So please do not leave me all on my own -
Come out once more and guide me the way home.

Eleanor Rudge

THE EXILE

With stealthy tread he pads the forest shades,
Merely a rustle in the waving grass
Bears witness to his passage through the glades.
Little shows of where he was want to pass.
How then came this intruder of the night to have strayed so far
From a warmer land?
Which once had been his national right,
Where the blue tropics seas lap golden sand,
With game abounding to provide his food.
Alas, this fine beast was captured and caged,
Imprisoned in quarters dark and crude.
Then carried back to this land so sad, enraged.
The lonely creature was yet unknown to me
Although he roamed the darkness he was free.

David Jennings

I WONDER

Will they find a cure for deadly ills?
Will outer space be every day travel?
Will the air be clean to breathe our fills?

Will the pen rule or the sword that kills?
Will democracy all the world's troubles unravel
Will they find a cure for deadly ills?

Will everyone have a life that fulfils?
Will some warmonger with us a war saddle?
Will the air be clean to breathe our fills?

Will the green belt be filled with over spills?
Will the brown sites be left just tarmac and gravel?
Will they find a cure for deadly ills?

Will more people have to learn new skills?
Will more work from home or have more miles to travel?
Will the air be clean to breathe our fills?

Will new crops, new seeds be sown in desert drills?
Will inventions all eyes and hearts marvel?
Will they find a cure for deadly ills?
Will the air be clean to breathe our fills?

Leslie Moate

GERRY ATTERICK

I doubt I'll ever be a famous man;
I'm old in years and soft in brain today.
Is it too bad to be an also-ran?

I've seldom done those things which laws do ban
And I have done my best and had my say.
I doubt I'll ever be a famous man.

Two stalwart sons do better than I can
In many things involved in work and play.
Is it too bad to be an also-ran?

Although I've had my moments in life's plan
Which won some plaudits and the odd hooray,
I doubt I'll ever be a famous man.

Few deeds did earn those words, éclat, élan;
Were I a god I would have feet of clay.
Is it too bad to be an also-ran?

One thing stands out since my review began;
My striving brought much fun along the way.
I doubt I'll ever be a famous man;
Is it too bad to be an also-ran?

Frank Sutton

HOW SILLY - HOW TRUE

How silly - how true
Day is given me God by You
Yet it's I who makes it
While it's You who takes it
In doing what You do.

Life, the wonder of You
Taking from and giving too
Loving us each minute
How silly - how true.

Always we're in Your view
Whilst giving us a day anew
Love, essential item of Your kits
And I too love You to bits.
My day, weaving its way to You
How real - how true.

Barbara Sherlow

BLUE, OH SO BLUE

Blue oh so blue what's in thy name
Chelsey - 'Y' is it not thee same
Brother's chant supports thou superior team
Echo shatter's small child's slumber dream

'Wise' one wine's 'Flo' atomic aim
Painted picture magnify thou fame
Majestic stars, child's playful scream
Blue oh so blue.

Misguided handball watery red shame
Child fair of peachy skin fragile frame
Soft face smiles sapphires dancing gleam
Proud defiant who hath reign supreme
Chelsea - 'A' final whistle in the game
Blue oh so blew!

Hazel Smith

I Did My Best

I did My best with pen in hand,
To write with words that would sound grand,
And so inspire the flow of verse,
Hoping the fear of failure to disperse,
Upon the whispering, shifting sand.

Sand of words scattered o'er the land,
That I can only watch and stand,
Hoping not to make this rhyme worse,
I did My best.

Words flowed sweetly from My pen and
Like haunting music by singer and band,
Filled My heart and let Me nurse,
The thought of achievement without a curse,
Now mindful of words left unwritten, unplanned,
I did My best.

Pamela Eckhardt

NO ONE RECALLS

No one recalls life in the womb
Or life remembers in the tomb,
Our mem'ry chips on input feed
And neural nets renewal need:
The slate starts clean with each new broom.

Can mem'ries new old tales resume
And voices from the past subsume?
Was mankind once a happy breed?
                    No one recalls.

This world is not all doom and gloom,
Both warp and weft knits up Fate's loom.
We crave life's plums but in our greed
Forget the stone contains the seed:
Were deserts once where flow'rs now bloom?
                    No one recalls.

Aubrey Woolman

VAINLY WE STRIVE

(A Rondeau)

Vainly we strive if star-crossed we were born,
ev'ry endeavour subjected to scorn.
Fickle Fortuna withholding a boon,
lost in the evening the gains won at noon:
for each rose we've plucked, a wound by a thorn,
past inner conflicts our strained nerves have torn:
Failed by false friends and by foes now forsworn,
youthful ambition a punctured balloon,
vainly we strive.

Knowing no laurels our brow will adorn,
stubborn, we cling to a hope most forlorn:
Bleak tho' in future our prospects may loom
(history warns us we should that assume)
adamant ever as rocks at Cape Horn,
vainly we strive.

T C Hudson

THE LONDON EYE

The eye is blind, it cannot see;
An engineering odyssey,
A massive wheel, contrived, aligned,
Conveying gawping humankind
To stare at London's majesty.

High up above the tallest tree,
Cameras on infinity,
A stunning view; yet they will find
        The eye is blind.

With photogenic irony
And middle class complacency
They miss the vagrant caked in grime,
Polluted air, violent crime,
The sleazy streets. They do not see
        The eye is blind.

Valerie Sutton

ON THE DIFFICULTY OF GETTING A LITTLE SCIENCE INTO A POEM

You can't explain what everybody knows
or replicate the obvious to those
who may be well aware, eg, that time
is quite unlike an ever-rolling stream
and quanta (pace Einstein) do play dice.

Unwise to speculate about black holes
or try to state what Gödel's Theorem shows.
Best not to touch on any suchlike theme
you can't explain.

Besides, a poem should not sermonise;
the reader hopes to get, with mild surprise,
a fresh perspective on a common scene.
Forget the science and try another scheme,
the world is full of mundane mysteries
you can't explain.

Tony Sumner

RONDEAU

So now I know: the rondeau is
A very Gallic artifice
And whether it be right or not
To squeeze it in an English pot
That's not a test I'd want to miss.

So, stifle cries of cowardice,
And, very like, of prejudice,
And hearken to the polyglot,
        Who now knows.

For it must always be remiss
To hover on a precipice
And good to be a patriot
Who takes the risk of writing rot
Or meeting there his Nemesis,
        As now he knows.

Denis Mann

GROWING OLD

I'm growing old, and now I fear
my mind will fog and every year
more names will slip from familiar faces,
more memories fade from all those places
that yesterday were sharp and clear.

I cannot see so well, nor hear
every word, and - oh dear!
I cannot reach to tie my laces:
I'm growing old.

Although to the world I may appear
over the hill and fighting a rear -
guard action to keep the traces
of youthful looks and hard-won graces,
it's hard to believe and hard to bear:
I'm growing old.

Jackie Hinden

HOW LIGHT HER STEP!

How light her step for middle years,
He has left home, she shed no tears
Instead, spring-cleaned her nest and car,
Broadened range of her repertoire
And cleared limits to her frontiers.

Yesterday, pace kept in low gears
As puppets moved by puppeteers,
Now hopes to be a late scholar.
How light her step!

Today, radiant smile appears
Once lost confidence reappears,
Her psyche was dried as cigar
Moistened, revived a dancing star
Beneath encasement of veneers.
How light her step!

Hilary Jill Robson

ALWAYS THE SAME

Always the same, you make me feel.
Moist, fast, uncovered stone, surreal
Partners. Like chalk and cheese, mould
Me to the artist I am sold.
Your able abyss I must steal

Hoodlum smile induced walk, the deal.
Your quiver makes the shiver real.
Transparent need, greed, turns you cold.
       Always the same.

How long the string, your heart to heal?
Not mirrored by unsighted zeal.
Under window, from bush words told,
Allows me to your claret fold.
No strings, did not listen, wax seal.
       Always the same.

David J Ratcliffe

HOW SWEET THE KISS

How sweet the kiss that tenderly
The mother gives as, smiling, she
Enfolds her newborn. As he grows
This tender sign of love he knows
From playmate, friend and family.

Then in youth's eager passion he
With lover joins in ecstasy,
And to her trembling senses shows
How sweet the kiss.

Then dandling children on his knee,
Gives these soft tokens lovingly,
That, when in death his eyes they close,
And on his coffin lay the rose,
This their fond requiem shall be.
How sweet the kiss.

Jackie Lapidge

When Old Age Comes

When old age never comes alone
It always tends to bring a moan
Whatever age you may be
You will still want a cup of tea
Or even have an ice cream cone

We all depend upon the phone
Especially if we live alone
Or if you even fear like me
When old age comes

You may be Derby . . . you may be Joan
Whatever your name you often moan
If you cannot always see
You still enjoy a cup of tea
We hear the words and then we groan
When old age comes.

Christine McCrae

London's Thames

I am the link that joins each part
from outer rim to city heart.
I flow in tidal majesty
past office block and dockland quay,
proud towered church and lively mart.

Fine bridges show designers' art,
roads follow where the Roman cart
once trundled with alacrity.
       I am the link.

Of sword and bomb, sturdy rampart,
anointed monarch, brash upstart,
ice fairs, beheadings, pageantry,
elections, riots, revelry
I have reflected history's chart.
       I am the link.

Beryl Cross

SURVIVAL?
(The Italian Sonnet)

We were living after the war, so they say,
men in the house went out picking up coal,
filling a sack full was always their goal,
people worked hard for low pay,
they caught tuberculosis and were taken away,
they said it was good for the soul,
children were taken round farms to
see the nice horse with its foal,
people looked forward and dreamed
of a much better day.

Now it is here we have more than our God to fear,
AIDS and mad cow have just taken a bow,
what they're doing to genes is not very clear,
and where some wish to go, they sniff dope in a row,
our Britain has never looked so grey and drear,
and soon we'll end up with the genes of a sow.

Jean Paisley

LIFE'S CHOICES

There is a path it's better not to tread.
A downward path for which there's only pain.
The innocence of youth sometimes misled,
Too late they realise, there is no gain.

There's a path of doubt and a path of greed,
The path of 'if only - now it's too late'.
A path of advice, we choose not to heed
And when life goes wrong, we blame it on fate.

There is a path, a wiser one to take,
Where loyalty, vision, hope, faith and truth,
Are some of life's choices we have to make,
To build on the dreams which inspired our youth.

Life is like paths of newly fallen snow,
The path we choose to tread, each step will show.

Betty M Varley

A REASON FOR LIVING

Each man shall have a reason for living,
Or every brain cell will never function.
We get more pleasure when we are giving,
Than in all our selfish deeds or action.
Clever men tell us how we all can think,
Yet they know not why men need to do it.
All the stress can take us to the brink,
For we are not sane without your spirit.
Who puts the evil and greed in our mind?
To cause every man your sorrow and pain.
Who made men behave, so good and so kind?
To other men, without no thought of gain.
The word of God is the truth to all men,
They did come from the Father in heaven.

F Schofield

ADORAMUS TE DOMINE

Gold sunrays glancing through the leafless trees,
Pale moonbeams shedding eerie light around.
Soft kisses of a warmly perfumed breeze,
Bright yellow daffodils that surf the ground.
Sweet scent of hyacinths and lilac pale,
A rose of singing red, aroma rare.
Wild birdsong pouring over hill and dale.
Drops splashing, sparkling from the fountain there
Hosting a rainbow in its diamond shower.
Grace of a gliding swan in liquid calm,
Sheer beauty bound within a single hour
Of nature's wonders, soothing like a balm.
Great cosmic Lover of mankind, we stand
In awe and wonder at your lavish hand.

Mary Pledge

A Scot's Sonnet (Flooers)

There is a plant an all dynamic flooer
By witches' thimbles - lupin - climin' vine
Oan yonder lea rig 'neath a drackie moor
Stout woolly thrissle (solitary) comes tae mind

The perching whinchat honours flourished breem
Their place of meeting mystery enhanced
Rose of Sharon - sweet briar - shepherd's purse
Combined in kindness lead lifes animated dance.

Fair gowan wi' poppy - a likely duo in the den
Hail Jenny's blue een ramp a'hint yon lair
The water wraith hersel' furiver gairds
Wild fire an' gollan - alas tae bloom nae mair.

In the natural world - 'neath a woodland roan
A strollin' singer composed his sandie poem.

Irene Gunnion

HIDDEN FEELINGS

It can be hard to a feeling hide
from time to time eyes meet
and the stand-offs you must abide
you know each other you can greet

But feelings of desire must wait
probably for an eternity and a day
but who knows what time will bring or fate
knowing one day you might be able to say

All the things your heart could only desire
and the emotions you've had to hold near
in all those years you could only him admire
because of being found out and that was your fear
you know you care for him deep down inside
you also know this feeling you shall have to hide.

J A Burkill

MILITANT PASSION

'We are at war by Helen brought.'
Spoke Priam: as the net pulled taut
He bade his soldiers stand their ground
As Greek and Trojan hacked around:
Wisdom is not cheaply bought.

Mark Antony played amorous sport
At Cleopatra's perfumed court;
The asp at queenly throat enwound:
        We are at war.

Romeo in cold frisson thought
Juliet in death's arms lay caught,
Her beauty entombed underground;
His suicide serves to expound
The lover's life is deadly short:
        We are at war.

Terry Smith

THERE IS A LOVE

There is a love that secret lies
Away from sharp and questing eyes,
It dares not come above the brink
For fear that others start to think
And build too much with wild surmise.

The last to guess the lows and highs
Must be the pair of smiling eyes;
So eyes that yearn can only blink.
There is a love.

To smile when all that's in you cries
To grasp and hold and catch the prize;
To climb so high and never sink
And tremble on the very brink,
But never wake the questing eyes.
There is a love.

Tony MacMillan

BLUE RONDO

I missed my chance, it slipped away
as I dithered and dreamt of 'might' or 'may'.
A voice within cried 'Go for it now,'
another said 'Don't, remember your vow.'
Yet it wasn't that, that made me stay

but fear and inertia and cautious delay.
Lack of self-confidence, a compulsion to weigh
the odds each time I play, that's how
I missed my chance

to turn fond friendship's brightest ray
into - well, it didn't happen, so who's to say?
It's no big deal, not life or death, or slough
of despond. I'm fine - really! No funereal brow,
just a few waves of regret that break to betray
how I missed my chance.

Mike Robson

GENEROSITY

Just look around yourself and you will see
So many people fight over small things
If they acted out generosity
They would witness the happiness it brings

If we treated each other with respect
And realised that poverty does exist
So did not pursue Third World countries' debts
Ties between nations would be tightly fixed

We should celebrate beauty from within;
The gleaming beauty from a person's heart
Know that to be greedy is an evil sin:
Whilst being kind is a magnificent art

Remember to give back more than you take
Because this shield of greed we need to break.

Saqib Hussain Malik

FLOWERS

How could our years be better strewn and blessed
And would we feel bereft of light and scent?
Colour drenching fields, woods and rocky crest,
The childhood places where our footsteps bent.

Can painter's palette find that perfect blue
Or hint of mystic beauty in one flower?
The earth is full of every rainbow hue
And redolent of nature's hidden power.

Absorb with inner eye the symmetry
The perfect colour of a single rose,
Or feel delight in every flowering tree
And there where small and humblest wildflower grows.

Be glad and sing a psalm of thankful praise
For pure and sensual pattern of our days.

Joan Perry

ABNEGATION

Love, all unbidden, knocked upon my door . . .
I knew - alas - I dare not let him in;
He stormed my heart, but I was free no more -
I could not wait forever on Fate's whim.

He long remained, convinced that he would win . . .
Of his persuasion, he was oh, so sure!
He did not dream that I might not give in,
He thought he held the key to my heart's core -

That, at a word, I'd run, forgetting all
To taste of joys that he, alone, could bring . . .
But I resisted Love's seductive call,
Despite the pain, which, to my soul still clings.

But guilt stains not, my proud, unsullied hearth
While hope's bright flame rekindles . . . in my heart.

Elizabeth Amy Johns

ANCHOR BOOKS
SUBMISSIONS INVITED
SOMETHING FOR EVERYONE

ANCHOR BOOKS GEN - Any subject,
light-hearted clean fun, nothing unprintable
please.

THE OPPOSITE SEX - Have your say on the
opposite gender. Do they drive you mad or can
we co-exist in harmony?

THE NATURAL WORLD - Are we destroying
the world around us? What should we do to
preserve the beauty and the future of our planet -
you decide!

All poems no longer than 30 lines.
Always welcome! No fee!
Plus cash prizes to be won!

Mark your envelope (eg *The Natural World)*
And send to:
Anchor Books
Remus House, Coltsfoot Drive
Woodston, Peterborough, PE2 9JX

**OVER £10,000 IN POETRY PRIZES
TO BE WON!**

Send an SAE for details on our New Year 2000
competition!